Simple Gospel

Gospel

How Your Christian Life Is Really Supposed to Work

Simply

Grace

Study Guide

Bob Christopher

Excerpts from Simple Gospel Simply Grace (ISBN 978-0-736962-72-8) used with permission from Harvest House Publishers, Eugene, OR.

Simple Gospel Simply Grace Study Guide

Copyright © 2015 Basic Gospel, Inc., Lewisville, TX 75057
ISBN 978-1-931899-40-6

Printed in the United States of America.

Contents

GOD'S GUY

The first day of my freshmen year in college, I made a vow to God. It went something like this: "God, I know I've been a disappointment to you. Thank you for a clean slate and for the opportunity to start fresh in college. From this day forward, I promise to be your guy."

What types of promises have you made to God? What was the motivation for those promises?

Were you able to live up to your promises to God?

Have you ever asked God for a fresh start in life? If so, what did you hope would change in your life?

Romans 7:18 reads, "I have the desire to do what is good, but I cannot carry it out."

Has this ever described your experience as a Christian? How did you try to change so that you could carry out what was good?

I shared that I felt sin was having its way in my life, and that I didn't seem to have a choice in the matter.

Have you ever reached that point in your life? How did you handle that reality?

Paul had some very strong words for the Galatians. He wrote, "How foolish can you be? After starting your Christian lives in the Spirit, why are you now trying to become perfect by your own human effort?" (Galatians 3:3)

In what ways have you applied human effort to the Christian life? What were the results?

Are you willing to admit that human effort — the path of trying harder, doing better, and being better — is not the way to live the Christian life?

Nagging Questions

I describe my first encounter with grace this way: "Earlier that morning, I hadn't been thinking about spiritual things. I wasn't praying for God to do a work in my life. It just happened. Christ's death for me became real. It pushed its way into my heart and soul and brought to life my need for Christ."

Describe your first grace encounter; the point in time when your need for Christ became real.

What aspect of the Gospel message captured your heart and mind at that time?

The verse that best described my first grace encounter is Romans 5:8: "God demonstrates his own love for us in this: While we were still sinners, Christ died for us."

What verse best describes your first grace encounter?

Even though I understood my need for Jesus, I didn't know the true depth of my need. As a result, I developed some faulty beliefs about Christianity and about being a Christian. One of those was the idea that Christianity was a self-improvement program.

What are some of the faulty beliefs you have held concerning Christianity?

My faulty beliefs about the Christian life left me with two nagging questions — 1) How can I call myself a Christian but experience so little power for change? 2) How can I be so sincere and eager yet struggle so much with temptation?

Have you ever struggled with these two questions?

What answers have you found?

Grace Defined

Martyn Lloyd-Jones wrote, "The Christian life starts with grace, it must continue with grace, it ends with grace." The Christian life is simply grace from start to finish.

In your own words, define grace.

One of the most famous passages in the Bible is Ephesians 2:8, 9: "By grace you have been saved through faith. And this is not your own doing; it is the gift of God, not a result of works, so that no one may boast."

According to this passage, how are we saved?

According to John 1:14, is there any way to separate grace from the person and work of Jesus Christ?

According to the following passages, how does the grace of God benefit you?

Ephesians 1:7–8

Ephesians 4:4–5

Titus 2:11–14

Acts 20:32

Romans 6:14

1 Corinthians 15:10

2 Corinthians 12:9

Based on these passages, write a new definition of grace.

How does this definition compare to the one you wrote earlier?

Far too often, Christians think of grace as merely a covering for their past sins.

How would this idea hinder someone from experiencing the full benefits of grace here and now?

Grace is active in our present and moves us into our future. I've defined it as God's work in Jesus to make us spiritually alive and to empower us to live in this world as his children.

This grace is not only the means of salvation; it is the way of the Christian life. Once grace starts in a person's life, it never quits. The simple gospel is simply grace. As you work through the pages of this study guide, you will find that grace packs all the power you need for life and godliness.

Are you ready to explore and discover the way of grace for your life?

> "The Christian life starts with grace, it must continue with grace, it ends with grace."
> Martin Lloyd-Jones

$$1$$

First Things First

The resurrection of Jesus Christ is the hinge on which the Christian faith hangs. Without it, Christianity would not exist. This is the sticking point for the critics and skeptics. They laugh and jeer at Christians for believing such nonsense. But it did happen. Jesus was raised from the dead. We believers stake everything on this one historical fact. Let's find out why.

In Luke 9:22, what did Jesus predict would happen to him?

After Jesus died and was buried, women went to the tomb to anoint his body with spices. What does Luke record they said when they arrived? (Luke 24:2)

Two men appeared to these women. What did these men say to the women and what did they ask the women to remember? (Luke 24:6-8)

Did the women remember that Jesus had predicted his resurrection from the dead?

The women told the disciples "all these things." In Luke 24:23, what exactly did the women say to the disciples?

Did the disciples believe what the women told them? (Luke 24:37-38)

What does Luke say that Jesus did for the disciples and what did Jesus tell them? (Luke 24:45-47)

So how do we know that Jesus was indeed raised from the dead? Who were and are the witnesses of this truth? (Luke 24:48)

In his letter to the Corinthians, Paul passed on to them things of first importance. What were those things according to 1 Corinthians 15:3-4?

How were these facts verified? (1 Corinthians 15:5-8)

According to 1 Corinthians 15:15, what did these witnesses testify about? If Christ had not been raised from the dead, what would we conclude about their credibility?

Paul wrote, "And if Christ has not been raised, your faith is futile; you are still in your sins" (1 Corinthians 15:17). What does this statement say about the significance of the resurrection for you?

First Life

The resurrection of Jesus Christ is the heart and soul of Christianity because it solves our deepest problem. Let's take a look at what the Bible says about our deepest need.

In Genesis 2:17, what did God say would happen to Adam and Eve if they ate of the tree of the knowledge of good and evil?

In Genesis 3:1-5, how did the serpent engage Eve in conversation about that forbidden tree?

What did the serpent help her conclude about the tree? (Genesis 3:6)

As a result, what did both Adam and Eve do?

What happened to them? (Genesis 3:7)

How did they respond to God and why? (Genesis 3:8-10)

Did they die physically that day? If not physically, what type of death did they experience?

> A miracle of new life occurs every time someone turns to Christ by faith. That is the power of the gospel, the amazing grace God pours out on those who look to him for life.

Adam and Eve ate from that tree, and they died. Not physically—Adam lived to the ripe old age of 930. The death they experienced was spiritual. The relationship they enjoyed with God was now gone. The life he had breathed into them vanished. They became fallen human beings. Here is the bad news about that event. The consequences of their decision affected you. What they became after the fall, they passed on to you.

In Romans 5:12, Paul tells us that sin and death entered the world through Adam. How many people did this affect?

How does Paul describe fallen man's spiritual condition in Ephesians 2:1?

Like Adam and Eve after the fall, you came into the world alive physically, but dead to God spiritually. What are some of the symptoms of spiritual death? How does it show up in our lives?

If spiritual death is our fallen condition, what then is our greatest need?

In John 10:10, why did Jesus come to earth?

What is the offer of the Gospel according to John 5:21?

If Christ had not been raised from the dead, could he offer eternal life to us?

What is God's act of grace for us according to Ephesians 2:4-5?

To be saved by grace means you have been made alive with Jesus Christ. Just as he was physically resurrected, you have been given new life. You were dead, and now you are alive in him.

2

The 180

Life is pretty good in the United States. As citizens, we are free to pursue happiness and live out our dreams. As a nation, Christianity is deeply woven into the fabric of our culture, but often only as an ideology that enriches our way of life. We look to God to improve our current situation and to make our lives better. We believe if we live by his rules and regulations and follow his principles, everything will work out fine for us. Sadly, this viewpoint reduces Christianity to nothing more than a self-improvement plan.

Christianity is not a self-improvement program. God doesn't improve the old. He gives you something brand new. Let's take a fresh look and see what Paul learned about this new life that is lived by grace through faith.

> Grace moves our thoughts and beliefs to the right place and to the right person. This is repentance.

I Was Wrong

I had it all wrong about Christianity. I looked at it as a self-improvement program. If I followed his rules and regulations and followed his principles, everything would work out fine. But that's not Christianity.

> Have you ever had an experience in which you thought you were doing something right only to discover you were doing it all wrong? Describe that experience.

> In Philippians 3:4-6, what qualities and credentials did Saul (Paul) lean on for meaning and purpose to life?

> In your opinion, why did Saul consider persecuting the church something to boast about?

> Does it seem odd that he claimed to be faultless as to righteousness based on the law?

> Could it be that he had it all wrong as to God's purpose and plan?

> In Philippians 3:9, what was Paul relying upon to gain righteousness?

> In Romans 7:10, what was Paul relying upon to gain eternal life?

God doesn't want better people. He wants new people-people who are fully alive in Him.

> According to John 5:39-40, what did Jesus say people
> like Paul missed in their efforts to gain eternal life
> through obedience to the law?

A Change of Mind

Paul's thinking before encountering Jesus did not line up at all with
God's perspective. He knew the Old Testament, but missed the author
of those Scriptures. He embraced the law but was totally at odds
with its intended purpose. He was a staunch apologist for the Jewish
way of life but was blind to the real blessing of being a descendant of
Abraham.

Paul needed his mind changed, what the Bible calls repentance.

In Acts 9, Luke tells the story of Paul on the road to Damascus. In
verses 1-2, what was Paul's purpose in going to Damascus?

What happened to Paul along the way? (Acts 9:3-4)

Whom did he encounter? (Acts 9:5)

How did Jesus answer Paul's question, "Who are you Lord?" (Acts
9:5)

Paul once thought that persecuting the church was something
God condoned. How did this encounter with Jesus change his
thinking?

After the encounter with Jesus, Paul experienced blindness for three days. What happened to him after those three days? (Acts 9:17-18)

Almost immediately he began to preach in the synagogues in Damascus. What was his message to his Jewish friends? (Acts 9:20-22)

This Damascus road experience was a moment of clarity for Paul. Jesus was not the renegade Paul thought that he was. No, Jesus was and is both Lord and God. This encounter turned Paul from unbelief to belief—a complete 180-degree turn, not only in his recognition that Jesus is God, but also in his understanding of the plan of God.

In Romans 7:9-11, what happened to Paul when he understood the significance of the commandment?

The commandment Paul refers to in this passage is "Do not covet." How did sin use this commandment in Paul and what was the result?

What did Paul conclude concerning the purpose of the law according to 2 Corinthians 3:6?

He once thought the law was intended to bring life, but then he had a change of mind when he saw the real plan of God in the Gospel. How does Paul explain the Gospel in 1 Corinthians 15: 3-4?

What is the lead event in the Gospel story? Why is this important to understand?

How did Paul describe this Gospel story taking place in his life according to Galatians 2:19-20?

Without death, there can be no resurrection. Paul learned this truth. He embraced his spiritual death. He saw his helplessness and his hopelessness. He let go of his self-effort. He let go of his self-righteousness. He let go of his status as a Pharisee. He took hold, or better yet, the Gospel took hold of him. Jesus's love, grace and mercy turned this blasphemer into a preacher, changed an enemy into a friend, and transformed the "chief of sinners" into a saint. This is the power of the Gospel of Jesus Christ.

A Happy Ending

One of the last miracles Jesus performed occurred in the tiny village of Bethany, and it involved three of his most beloved followers— Mary, Martha and Lazarus. Lazarus was near death. His condition was serious. Martha and Mary sent an urgent word to Jesus asking him to come quickly. They were hoping for and expecting a miracle. But their hopes were dashed. Jesus didn't arrive on time. And when he did arrive, Lazarus had already been in the tomb four days. Jesus intentionally stayed away, but he had a reason.

When Jesus did arrive, what did Martha say to him? (John 11:21)

Based on her response, did she think Jesus could do anything for her brother once he died?

In John 11:25-26, what did Jesus claim about himself?

After making this claim, what did he ask Martha?

How did he prove his statement to Martha, Mary and those who were with them in Bethany? (John 11:41-44)

With this miracle, what do you think Jesus was teaching us about the nature of Christianity?

Jesus could have healed Lazarus. He could have done so long-distance simply by speaking a word. But Jesus had something else in mind. And he wants you to have something else in mind. God doesn't want better people. He wants new people—people who are fully alive in him.

Are you willing to place all that you are in the hands of Jesus, the one who is the resurrection and the life?

Paul's 180 is a sterling example to us all of the amazing power of God's grace. Jesus's love and mercy turned a blasphemer into a preacher, changed an enemy into a friend, and transformed the chief of sinners into a saint. This is the power of the gospel.

3

The Essence of Faith

Every great game, invention, or field of study has someone that stands as the father of that particular endeavor. James Naismith was the father of basketball; Hippocrates, the father of modern medicine and Adam Smith, the father of modern economics.

The same is true for the story of faith. The story starts with Abraham. Yes, there were others, such as Abel, Enoch and Noah, who lived long before Abraham and were commended for their faith. Yet, it is in the life of Abraham we see the essence of faith. Paul describes him as "the father of all who believe" (Romans 4:11).

Since the Bible tells us that we are saved by grace through faith, it's important for us to take a look at the father of faith.

The Promise

Abraham—Abram at the time—along with his family set out from Ur to find a new home. They stopped in Harran. There, God spoke to Abraham.

In Genesis 12:1, what did God ask Abraham to do?

What four promises did God make to Abraham? (Genesis 12:2-4)

How did Abraham respond?

What does this teach you about the essence of faith?

Abraham's family traveled until they arrived in the land of Canaan. What promise concerning this land did God make to Abraham? (Genesis 12:7)

God promised Abraham that the world would be blessed through his son. How did he fulfill this promise according to 1 Peter 1:3-4?

The same is true of you. God showed up in your story. He spoke promises and blessings into your life through the person and work of Jesus Christ.

Let's stop here to examine the key elements of the story thus far. The dominant figure in the story is God. He is the main character, not Abraham. He intentionally reached out to Abraham and inserted himself into Abraham's story to make Abraham a part of his story. Notice how God entered the scene—not with condemnation and wrath, but with promises and blessings. This is grace in action. This grace compelled Abraham to be a willing participant.

How does Abraham's story relate to yours?

Abraham did have a concern that he shared with God. He was childless and wondered about who would inherit his estate. How did God answer this concern? (Genesis 15:4-5)

What was Abraham's response? (Genesis 15:6)

What did God credit to his account?

In what way does Paul in Romans 4:23-24 relate Abraham's response of faith to you?

The Test

God did deliver on his promise to Abraham. When Abraham was 100, his wife, Sarah, gave birth to a son and they named him Isaac. "Some time later," as Genesis 22 begins, God tested Abraham.

What did God tell Abraham to do with Isaac? (Genesis 22:2)

What was Abraham's response? (Genesis 22:3)

Put yourself in Abraham's shoes. How do you think you would have responded to God's command to sacrifice Isaac?

What do you think was going through Abraham's mind?

The New Testament writers clue us in. In Romans 4:17, Paul wrote that Abraham believed God. What specifically did he say that God could do?

What did Abraham reason that God could do according to Hebrews 11:17-19?

What do these two passages say about the essence of Abraham's faith?

The Moment

After a three day journey, Abraham and Isaac arrived at Mount Moriah, the place of sacrifice. The day had come. It was time for Abraham to do what God had ordered.

Abraham bound Isaac and laid him on the altar. As Genesis 22:10 reads, Abraham grabbed the "knife to slay his son." Could you do it? Could you take the life of your son of promise?

What have you learned about Abraham's faith that enabled him to carry out God's command?

According to Genesis 22:11-13, what happened at this point?

What did Abraham call that particular place? (Genesis 22:14)

How did the Lord provide for you according to John 1:29?

When told to take Isaac's life, Abraham reasoned that God had the power to raise him back to life. How was his faith rewarded according to Hebrews 11:19?

Abraham was tested. at the critical moment, his faith proved genuine. He truly believed God had power over death. In Romans 10:8-9, what does God ask you to believe?

Here is where belief in the resurrection is crucial. Do you genuinely believe that God has the power to give you new life in Jesus Christ?

Resurrection defies human reason and logic, but so does God. He is the God who gives life to the dead. Here are the facts. Three days after Jesus's body was laid in a borrowed tomb, God raised him from the dead. Let me ask:

Do you really believe this to be true? Has it captured your heart and soul?

> Here is where belief in the resurrection is crucial. If you do not believe God raised Jesus from the dead, you're not going to believe he can give you a new life.

If not, perhaps it's time for you to step into the faith of Abraham and experience the reality of the resurrection.

4

The Crossover

What happens to a person when he responds to the Gospel through faith? He crosses over from death to life, just as Jesus said. "Very truly, I tell you, whoever hears my word and believes him who sent me has eternal life and will not be judged but has crossed over from death to life" (John 5:24). This is what happens to anyone who trusts in Jesus. Let's take a closer look.

The Wrong Place

Before you trusted Jesus Christ and were made alive in him, you were not where you were supposed to be. You were in the wrong place.

In Genesis 2:15, where did God put Adam to live? For what purpose?

Were Adam and Eve able to stay in the Garden after they had eaten the fruit of the tree of the knowledge of good and evil? (Genesis 3:23-24)

Once banished, did Adam and Eve have access to the tree of life?

Adam and Eve's act doomed us all to the wrong place. How did Jesus describe that place in John 12:46?

Have you ever felt as if you weren't where you were supposed to be in life?

What is Jesus's promise to those who follow him in John 8:12?

According to 1 Peter 2:9, what does God call us out of?

Where does he place us?

How does Paul describe this in Colossians 2:13?

Based on the above passages, where is the right place for us to be?

> To cross over from death to life
> is to cross from darkness to light.

The Wrong Person

Darkness is ruled by dark forces. Contrary to what we think, no one is independent or free. Everyone is under the control of someone else.

According to Ephesians 2:2, when you lived in the dark, what shaped your way of life?

Who sets the agenda in the dark?

What characteristic does the "ruler of the kingdom of the air" cultivate in those who live in the dark?

How does John describe those who do what is sinful? (1 John 3:8)

Why does he say that they are of the devil?

In 1 John 2:16, what are the ways of the world?

Do any of these qualities of the world come from God?

When Jesus rescued you, he set you free from the world system. How does Acts 26:18 describe this transformation?

In Romans 8:14, who leads the children of God?

> To cross over from death to life
> is to cross over from bondage to freedom.

The Wrong Purpose

One of the big three questions we ask is, "Why am I here?" This is a question about purpose. In the realm of darkness, purpose is where we miss the mark. We don't live out God's desires for us. Instead, we live for ourselves.

In Ephesians 2:3, what does Paul say we once lived to gratify?

Does this sound like God's purpose for our lives?

In the book of Ecclesiastes Solomon wrote that "everything is meaningless." Has there been a time in your life you felt this way? If so, describe what you were experiencing?

In Philippians 2:13, who is at work in us?

For what purpose?

In light of this truth, what do you think it means to work out your salvation with fear and trembling? (Philippians 2:12)

How does Peter say we live our lives in 1 Peter 4:2-3?

To cross over from death to life
is to cross over to a new purpose in life.

The Wrong Identity

There is something else that Adam handed down to us—the wrong identity.

In Romans 5:19, what were we made through the disobedience of Adam?

What was your identity before you crossed over from death to life?

Was this truth difficult for you to admit?

What does 1 Timothy 1:15 tell us about why Jesus came into the world?

In light of this verse, why was it important for you to admit the truth that you were a sinner?

According to John 1:12-13, what did you become the moment you received Jesus Christ and were born of God?

What is your new identity in Christ?

In 1 John 3:1-3, what compelled God the Father to change our identity from sinner to child of God?

What will we discover about ourselves when Jesus Christ appears?

How does this hope shape the way we live here and now?

> To cross over from death to life
> means crossing over to a brand new identity.

The Bridge

Jesus Christ bridges the gap between death and life. We cross over through him. There is no other way. That sounds exclusive and certainly politically incorrect. But it is also the most loving thing you or I can say. Life is found in Jesus Christ—nowhere else.

According to 1 John 5:11-12, what did God give you?

Where is this eternal life?

If you have the Son, what do you have?

What about those who do not have the Son?

What did Jesus claim about himself in John 14:6?

Is there any other way to the Father except through Jesus?

Jesus Christ is the way out of death into life. He is the way out of darkness into light. He is the cure the world needs.

Here is the good news. If you have confessed with your mouth that Jesus is Lord and have believed in your heart that God raised him from the dead, you too have crossed over from death to life. You have received the cure.

That's news worth shouting from the rooftops.

$$5$$

Great Expectations

Through faith in Jesus Christ, you crossed over from death to life.

And something else happened as well. God found a home in you. This is a story line that runs through the Bible. Think about the tabernacle Moses built and the temple Solomon built. God filled them with his presence, as evidenced by fire and smoke. These were striking and powerful images, but they were shadows of God's real plan. That plan is the story of Pentecost.

Here's What Happened

Sadly, many see salvation as nothing more than a golden ticket that will grant them entry into heaven when they die. Yes, we are immediately present with the Lord when we die. That's only part of the story. Salvation is God's act of grace to make us spiritually alive. And something else happens as well.

In Acts 1:4-5, what command did Jesus give to his disciples?

What was going to happen to them?

What else did Jesus say about the promise in Acts 1:8?

In Acts 17:24, what did Paul explain to the Athenians about God's dwelling place?

The day of Pentecost was marked by strange occurrences—a loud rushing wind, tongues of fire, and people from different countries hearing the wonders of God in their native languages. How did Peter explain these strange events? (Acts 2:14-17)

Peter then preached the very first evangelistic message about the death, burial and resurrection of Jesus. At the end, he encouraged the people to repent and be baptized. To those who believed the message, what would they receive? (Acts 2:38)

How does Paul describe what happens at salvation in Colossians 1:27?

What are believers called in 1 Corinthians 3:16 and why?

On the day of Pentecost, God dedicated his temple—the body of Christ—and filled it with his presence. You were added to that temple the day you believed and received Jesus Christ and were indwelled by God's Spirit.

Take time and think through the ramifications. God's presence in your life changes everything. The God of the universe is living in you. His love, grace, truth and power are now coursing through your spiritual veins.

Now all your hopes and expectations for life are pinned to him. Jesus showed up in your life. He is on the scene. As a result, you can live with great expectations.

Assurance of Salvation

Many verses in the Bible make the case for eternal security. The strongest come from the mouth of Jesus.

What did Jesus say about those who hear his voice and follow him in John 10:28-30?

Will those who have eternal life ever perish?

Who protects us and keeps us eternally secure?

Who else?

Do you know of anyone or anything powerful enough to snatch you out of the hand of God?

In 1 John 5:11-13, what is the testimony that the Apostle John gives to us?

Where is this eternal life found?

So, if you have the Son, what do you have?

Why did John give this testimony? (verse 13)

According to Romans 8:15-16, how does the Holy Spirit assure you that you belong to Christ?

Are you getting the idea that God wants you to know you are saved? It is so important to him that he asked the Spirit to make this truth real in your heart. Your assurance of salvation is on his shoulders and he is up to the task.

With Christ living in you, you can walk in assurance.

> Saying yes to God's Spirit
> means you will not carry out the desires of the flesh.
> With Christ in you, you can say no to sin.

Say No to Sin

Yes, I am saying you can expect to say no to sin as a believer in Christ. Many try and many fail, but they go about it the wrong way. They rely on willpower and sheer grit to withstand the onslaught. That is a strategy that will never work.

Saying no to sin is the result of the Holy Spirit's work in your life. This is grace in action.

In Titus 2:11-12, how does the grace of God instruct you to live as a child of God?

God's grace goes far beyond merely teaching you to say "no" to sin. What are the characteristics of this new life the grace of God works in you? (Titus 2:13-14)

What confidence can you have to overcome and live victoriously? (1 John 4:4)

How does Paul encourage you to live in Galatians 5:16?

What is the result of walking by the Spirit?

By walking in the Spirit, whose desires will you be carrying out?

Does walking in the Spirit mean you will not encounter temptation in life or have desires of the flesh?

Keeping in step with the Spirit is where you will find the real excitement in life. It's not out there in the world. It's in Jesus. So, what is the Holy Spirit working in your life right now?

One of the desires of the flesh is revenge. Describe how the Spirit of God would work in your life so that the desire for revenge would not be gratified. What is your role in that process?

What kind of qualities does the Spirit produce in your life according to Galatians 5:22?

In light of the fruit of the Spirit, how does Paul encourage us to live? (Galatians 5:25)

Saying yes to God's Spirit means you will not carry out the desires of the flesh. With Christ in you, you can say no to sin.

Bear Fruit

The pressures of life can do all sorts of things inside us. Fear and anger can fill our minds, and restlessness can disturb our souls. We get to the point where all we want is a little peace. But it's not out there in the world. And you can't buy it. Peace comes from God. As we learn to abide in Christ, we will bear the fruit of his peace in our lives.

Reread Galatians 5:22. Why do you think Paul describes these nine characteristics as the "fruit of the spirit"?

In John 15:5, what illustration did Jesus use to describe his relationship to us?

Who is the vine?

Who is the branch?

What role does the vine play?

What role does the branch play?

What is the result of the vine-branch relationship?

Is it possible for the branch to bear fruit apart from the vine?

Based on this illustration how can you experience peace and bear the fruit of the Spirit in your life?

Are you willing to abide in Jesus as the source of your life?

It seems simple, doesn't it? It is, because the real work is God's. We simply bear the fruit of his work in us. It is by grace through faith. With Christ in you, you will bear the fruit of his Spirit.

Are you a believer? Have you placed your full weight of trust in the one who died and rose again? If so, Jesus Christ has found a home in your heart. Expect him to do great things in and through you.

6

It Is Finished

Miroslav Volf, a theology professor at Yale, wrote this: "God is the God who forgives." We see the reality of this truth in Jesus's act of grace through death. Having said this, let me ask several questions.

Do you know that God has forgiven your sins? If not, do you long to know God's forgiveness? Do you want to experience rest and peace and assurance?

The Gospel proclaims that you can know and experience God's forgiveness. If you want to grow in your relationship with Jesus Christ and experience his love, the cross is the place to start. That all important question, "Will God forgive my sin?" is answered in the death of Jesus Christ.

How did Jesus say the greatest love of all is exemplified in John 15:13?

Based on Jesus's statement, why did Jesus die for you?

Three Observations Concerning Forgiveness

1. All Christians know that Christ died to forgive their sins.

2. Even with the clear declaration of God's Word that our sins-past, present and future-have been forgiven through the finished work of Jesus Christ, Christians still struggle with fear and guilt. They wonder whether they've been forgiven or not.

3. Confusion on this most fundamental truth hampers every other aspect of the Christian life.

Why the Cross?

Why did Jesus have to die? It was and is a puzzling question. With the right perspective the answer becomes clear. Let's take look.

In Matthew 16:21, what did Jesus explain to his disciples?

How did Peter respond? (verse 22)

What did Jesus say in response to Peter's bold assertion? (verse 23)

What point of view led Peter to take his stand to protect Jesus from impending death?

Would Peter have made this statement if he were looking at the cross from God's perspective?

According to Hebrews 9:22, why did Jesus have to die on our behalf?

Could we be forgiven of our sins apart from the shed blood of Jesus?

In Hebrews 10:7, what context did the writer give to the death of Christ?

> Jesus died to do the will of his Father. His death delivered forgiveness to you. There was no other way.

What does this say to you about God's will concerning the forgiveness of your sins?

His Final Steps

Jesus's final week began with his triumphant march into Jerusalem. The people laid palm branches at his feet and hailed him as their King. Their hallelujahs were short lived however. Later that week, Judas betrayed Jesus to the religious leaders, who arrested him in the Garden of Gethsemane. The high priest and elders interrogated Jesus, mocked him, and beat him through the night, hoping to find evidence to condemn him to death. Determined to find something, Caiaphas, the high priest, pressed Jesus concerning his identity.

In Matthew 26:63, what question did Caiaphas demand Jesus to answer?

How did Jesus answer? (verse 64)

What was the high priest's response? (verse 65)

Caiaphas appealed to the elders that were present, "What is your verdict?" What was their verdict concerning Jesus and the penalty they thought just?

Did they find him guilty of a crime?

The Jewish leaders needed the Romans to carry out the punishment. They sent Jesus to stand trial before Pilate. Pilate appealed Jesus's fate to the crowd. In Matthew 27:22, what did Pilate ask the crowd?

How did they respond? (verses 22-25)

In light of the crowd's demand, what did Pilate do? (verse 26)

Based on what Jesus told his disciples in Matthew 16:21, wasn't Pilate's cowardly act to hand Jesus over to be crucified the exact outcome that had to happen to carry out the plan and will of God on your behalf?

Calvary

Jesus was crucified between two criminals on a hill called Calvary. It was nine in the morning when the Romans soldiers nailed his hands and feet to the cross and then suspended him between heaven and earth.

At noon the sky darkened. It was the darkest moment in human history. How did Paul describe what was happening at that moment in 2 Corinthians 5:21?

Jesus hung on the cross for six hours. What did he cry out just before he died? (John 19:31)

At that point, had Jesus carried out the will of his Father?

How did God punctuate Christ's finished work? (Matthew 27:51-53)

What do his words mean to you?

How did John describe Jesus in John 1:29?

Did Jesus take away your sin at the cross?

Past, Present and Future

Peter was the first to preach the good news of Jesus to a Gentile audience. The sermon took place in Ceasarea in the home of Cornelius, a Roman centurion. Peter's message that day helps connect the dots from the cross to your day-to-day life.

Based on Peter's message and the testimony of the prophets of old, what did you receive the moment you believed in Jesus? (Acts 10:43)

According to Colossians 2:13, how many of your sins did Jesus forgive?

What does the word "all" mean to you? Does all include the sins you are yet to commit?

If your future sins were not included, what would need to happen for those sins to be forgiven? (Hebrews 9:22)

Was Jesus's death on the cross sufficient to take away all of your sins once and for all?

The writer of Hebrews states the case for our once-for-all forgiveness. In Hebrews 9:24, where did Christ enter on our behalf and who did he appear before?

In verse 25, how many times did he appear?

Why did he appear? (verse 26)

In verse 28, how many times did Christ die? How many sins did his sacrifice take away?

The writer of Hebrews tells us that Christ will come again. When Jesus does come again, is he coming to deal with our sins? Why not?

Why is Jesus coming again?

Based on Jesus's death on the cross, what did John say is true about your sins? (1 John 2:12)

> Let John's words encourage your heart: "I am writing to you, dear children, because your sins have been forgiven on account of his name" (1 John 2:12)

> As far as your sins are concerned, there is nothing left to be done. Jesus died once for all time. The gift of forgiveness you received at salvation is complete. Your sins have been forgiven because God is a God who forgives.

7

From Fear to Faith

Jesus's accomplishment on the cross means your sins are no longer an issue with God. They've been forgiven. Nothing more needs to be done.

From a human perspective, this doesn't sound right. Isn't there something more that needs to be done when we sin? The New Testament has much to say about this. The overwhelming evidence will move your heart from fear to faith.

What did Jesus cry out from the cross in John 19:30?

What do you think these three words mean?

How does the writer of Hebrews explain Jesus's victory cry in Hebrews 10:17-18?

Have your sins been forgiven?

What do you have in Christ according to Ephesians 1:7-8?

Is there any longer a need for another sacrifice for sin?

In light of this, how would you answer the question, "what am I supposed to do when I sin?"

Binaca

For a group of boys in a shoplifting gang, Binaca, a breath freshener, presented quite the challenge. I don't know why we stole this item. Maybe it presented a challenge—could we get away with it? I didn't. When I got caught, fear and guilt gripped my heart. I made restitution, but that didn't ease my sense of guilt. There was a bigger question.

What is God going to do with me? If you've never rested in the finished work of Jesus Christ, that is a scary thought. We all know intuitively that God cannot let sin go unpunished. Naturally, we start wondering if there is something that we can do to erase the black mark of sin beside our names and get back into God's good graces.

Here is how it worked for me. It started with a sin. That sin caused guilt and an intense fear of punishment. Out of this fear, I pleaded with God for forgiveness and promised him I would do better. And then the next sin came. I repeated the process over and over again, but I never felt forgiven. I had done my part, but I was never sure God had done his. My formula for forgiveness didn't ease the guilt or take away the fear.

> Let's get personal. Was there ever a time in your life when the fear of God's punishment overwhelmed you?

What did you do to try to turn God's punishment away?

Did your efforts rid you of the fear or erase your guilt?

What did John say was the remedy to our fear of God's punishment in 1 John 4:18?

What does it mean if you are still afraid?

Have you ever looked deep inside and recognized fear as the driving force in your life?

Are you willing to trust the love of God to turn your fear to faith?

> Fear turns grace into a reward.
> This is not the way of grace.

The Fear Factor

Being controlled by fear is devastating. It is the natural consequence of sin. We first see this in the Garden.

In Genesis 3:10, why did Adam and Eve hide from God after they had sinned?

What motivated their decision to hide?

Had they ever known fear like that before they sinned?

According to Colossians 1:21, what is it that makes us fearful of God and makes us enemies in our minds?

What is God's ultimate plan for us? (Colossians 1:22)

What does this say about God's disposition toward us?

How did God show that he was and is for us in 1 John 4:10?

An alternate rendering of 1 John 4:10 reads this way: "This is love: not that we loved God, but that he loved us and sent his Son as the one who would turn aside his wrath, taking away our sins."

Based on this rendering, who took the punishment you justly deserved?

Have your sins been judged and punished?

We experience salvation by grace through faith, and we experience forgiveness by grace through faith as well.

In what way does the love of God drive out your fear of punishment? (1 John 4:18)

What other fear does the love of God free you from in Hebrews 2:15?

What if you actually believed that God forgave your sins in Christ? What if you took your stand on the New Covenant, which includes

God's promise that he remembers your sins no more? What if you genuinely trusted in the blood of Christ shed for you once and for all?

From Fear to Faith

God did forgive your sins in Christ and He has made the choice to remember your sins no more. God's grace has been poured out on you in forgiveness. It is yours. Perhaps you are still struggling to believe this to be true for you and you can't let go of the idea that you need to do something to get back into God's good graces when you sin. Maybe this question will help you settle the issue once and for all: What does God do when you sin? Let's take a look at seven passages of Scripture to find out.

Look up each passage and then write down the action God takes on your behalf.

1 John 2:12

Romans 8:15-16

Romans 13:10 and Hebrews 12:10

Titus 2:11

Ephesians 4:22-24

Romans 8:28

Philippians 1:6

By grace, Jesus took your sins on himself. By grace, he suffered the punishment you justly deserved. By grace, he offered his blood to the Father on your behalf. By grace, he forgave your sins. Now through faith, thank Jesus for what he has done and rest confidently in the forgiveness that is yours in him.

Let the love of God turn your fear into faith.

8

They're All Gone

We've spent the past two chapters discussing forgiveness, but what does the word really mean? When you say your sins have been forgiven, what does that mean to you?

Let's start with your definition of forgiveness. What does this word mean to you?

The Merriam-Webster online dictionary defines forgiveness this way; to stop feeling anger toward (someone who has done something wrong): to stop blaming (someone): to stop requiring payment of (money that is owed).

How does your definition of forgiveness compare to the dictionary definition?

Who Can Forgive?

To find out what forgiveness really means, we need to go to the source, to the one who has the authority to forgive our sins.

> Read Mark 2:1-12. Why did the four men bring their friend to Jesus?

> How determined were they to get their friend in front of Jesus?

> The four men lowered their friend down through the roof right down in front of Jesus. When Jesus saw him, what did he say to him? (verse 5)

> Does Jesus's response seem strange to you? Was the paralytic there seeking forgiveness?

> What were the teachers and religious leaders thinking about Jesus's statement?

> What did they understand about forgiveness?

> Who is the only one with the authority and power to forgive sins?

> With Jesus's statement, what was he claiming about himself?

> According to verse 10, does Jesus have the authority to forgive sins?

What was the good news for the paralytic?

How did the crowd respond to Jesus's teaching?

To this paralytic, Jesus delivered his mercy with four simple words, "Your sins are forgiven." This is grace. Here is the good news. He says the same four words to you. These aren't just nice words to make you feel better about yourself. Jesus is God. When he says your sins are forgiven, they are forgiven.

Forgiveness Defined

What actually happens when God forgives? Let's find out by exploring the biblical concept of forgiveness.

The main Greek word for forgiveness is aphiemi. According to The Complete Word Study Dictionary, the primary meaning is "to send forth or away, to let go from oneself." It also means to dismiss, or put away; to let go from one's power or possession, to let go free, to remove; and to let go from one's further notice, care, attendance, occupancy—that is, to leave or let alone.

Based on this definition, let's ask this question. What does God do when he forgives our sins?

Off They Go!

In the Old Covenant sacrificial system, sins were ceremonially transferred to an animal that was to be sacrificed, such as a bull or goat.

What did this picture or foreshadow according to 2 Corinthians 5:21?

In exchange for our sins, what does Jesus make us?

What was the problem with the blood of bulls and goats in Hebrews 10:4, 11?

In 1 John 3:5, why did Christ appear?

Did Jesus take away your sins through his sacrificial death?

How far have they been removed from you according to Psalm 103:12?

Jesus removed your sins from you once and for all!.

On the Day of Atonement, the high priest, after sacrificing a bull to atone for his sins, would take two male goats from the community of Israel and cast lots to determine which goat to sacrifice and which goat to use as the scapegoat.

Once the lots had been cast, he would take the blood of the goat he slaughtered behind the curtain and sprinkle it on the mercy seat. Once this was done, the high priest presented the live goat. What happened with this scapegoat provides a vivid picture of what Christ's sacrifice did with your sins.

In Leviticus 16:21-22, what did the high priest do symbolically with the sins of the people?

After he placed the sins on the head of the goat, what did he then do with the goat?

Where did the sins of the people go?

This ritual was merely symbolic. These sacrifices never actually cleansed the people once and for all (Hebrews 10:2). Did the scapegoat actually take away the sins of the people?

How about the sacrifice of Jesus Christ?

Was his blood sufficient to send your sins away once and for all?

Jesus sent your sins away from you once and for all!

In Hebrews 10:17, what does God say about our sins and lawless acts?

How does he confirm this truth in Hebrews 10:18?

At Calvary, God did remember your sins. What did he do with your sins at the cross according to Romans 8:3?

He did this in order for what to be met in you?

If the righteous requirements of the law have been met in you, is there anything left for God to do with your sin?

One of the definitions of the Greek word for forgiveness is this: to let go from one's further notice, care, attendance, occupancy— that is, to leave or let alone. In what way does the promise of Hebrews 10:17 satisfy this definition?

Read Hebrews 11. In what way does this chapter show that God no longer remembers our sins?

Many Christians fear that when they stand before God, every sin, every evil thought and every evil desire will be broadcast for all creation to see. How does the truth of Hebrews 10:17 cast that fear away?

Jesus remembers your sins no more!

This is what God has done with your sins. He removed them from you and placed them on Christ. He sent them away through Christ's shed blood. And now, he remembers them no more! This is forgiveness. This is a gift of grace.

Forgiving Others

If God is the only one who has the authority and power to forgive sins, why does the Bible encourage us to forgive others who have sinned against us? That is a good question to think through.

What does Ephesians 4:32 encourage us to do as believers?

What is the encouragement in Colossians 3:13?

In both of these passages, what does Paul make clear concerning God's forgiveness of your sins?

The word translated forgiveness in these two passages is the Greek word charizomai. The root word is charis which means grace. God's act to forgive your sins therefore is an act of grace. How then are we to forgive those who have wronged us?

What is the basis of this act of grace toward others according to 2 Corinthians 5:19?

Who works this measure of grace in our hearts and empowers us to choose not to count people's wrongs against them?

What do we reflect to the world when we forgive as God in Christ forgave us?

As you can see, there is more to forgiveness than meets the eye. God has done a powerful work for you in Christ. Listen again to the words of Jesus to the paralytic. "Your sins are forgiven." This is Jesus's message to you.

9

Let Go

Have you ever met someone who says, "I know God has forgiven me, but I'm having a hard time forgiving myself." Maybe this is something you are struggling with. If so, you are not alone. Many people find it difficult to forgive themselves.

As we learned in chapter 8, forgiveness is not a human concept. It originated with God, because ultimately all sins are against him. It is his choice to forgive or not to forgive. He chose to forgive. That's grace. He did so through Christ's shed blood (Hebrews 9:22). Forgiveness is yours in Christ. As C.S. Lewis so eloquently stated, "I think that if God forgives us we must forgive ourselves."

But why do we have such a hard time applying his forgiveness to our lives? Why do we choose to live with guilt and shame and to allow self-condemnation to have such a stronghold on us? Why do we allow the sins of our past to tell us who we are today? Let's take a look at the root cause and then examine three specific areas that keep us from applying God's forgiveness to our lives.

What warning does Hebrews 12:15 give to us?

What happens when we fall short of the grace of God?

What does this bitterness cause?

Based on this verse, what is the reason we struggle with forgiving ourselves?

Do you think that someone who says they know God has forgiven them, but can't forgive themselves, really understands God's forgiveness?

What then is the solution to forgiving yourself?

> People who are struggling
> to forgive themselves are troubled.

I'm Basically Good

If you buy the premise that you are basically good, you will miss the grace of God. If you are fundamentally good, you don't need grace.

How does Jesus explode the myth that we are basically good in Mark 10:18?

What does Romans 3:10-12 say about the character of people apart from Jesus Christ?

How did the prophet Jeremiah describe the condition of man's heart apart from Christ? (Jeremiah 17:9)

Based on these passages, can any one of us claim that we are basically good?

Who does God justify or declare righteous in Romans 4:5?

Will people who see themselves as basically good ever seek to be justified by God?

In this world, many people rationalize their actions and spin their pasts in a way that puts them in the best possible light. In what ways does the "basically good" myth feed these actions?

In what ways does this premise keep a person from knowing and experiencing the forgiveness of God?

I've Crossed the Line

Some people believe their sin is so bad they have crossed a line and that they are beyond the reach of God's grace and forgiveness. If there is a line we could cross, how bad would we have to be to cross it?

In 1 Timothy 1:15, what did Paul say that he was?

What were the sins Paul was guilty of committing in 1 Timothy 13?

Did these sins move him beyond the reach of God's mercy?

Instead of punishment and wrath, what did God pour out on Paul? (1 Timothy 1:14)

Who did Christ come into the world to save? (vs 15)

Why did Paul share this about himself? (vs 16)

In Romans 5:20-21, what happens when sin increases?

Paul is not saying we should go out and sin more, as some would think. He is simply saying that God's grace is bigger and more powerful than your sin. In what way does the resurrection of Jesus Christ prove this to be true?

Was your sin able to keep Christ in the grave?

According to Romans 8:1, what is true of those who are in Christ?

If you believe your sins are so big that they have exhausted the supply of God's grace, you are doomed to a life of self-condemnation. You will miss the grace of God. Here is the good news. God's grace never runs out. It is a limitless supply, which means there is no line you can cross. There is no place you can be that God cannot reach you and pour out his grace and mercy on you. Are you willing to receive his grace and mercy and set your heart at rest in his presence?

I Am Unworthy and Unlovable

We've all heard the story of the prodigal son. He took his inheritance and set out to take on whatever the world threw at him. The world with all its seductive charms lured him into a life of recklessness and waste. It led to a place where he felt unworthy and unlovable. Many feel just like this prodigal son.

In Luke 15:18-19, the prodigal son prepared a speech to give to his dad. What was he going to say?

What was the reason he was going to ask his dad to make him like one of his hired servants?

When his father saw him, what happened? (Luke 15:20)

How did the father celebrate the son's return? (Luke 15:22-24)

Have you ever felt unworthy or unlovable?

What brought about those feelings?

Does God know all about you? Does he know your sins and the horrible things that have happened in your life?

God knows the truth about you, yet what did he choose to do on your behalf according to John 3:16?

In what ways does this powerful truth help a person step out from behind those feelings of unworthiness?

God knows your real story. He is not ashamed of you. For proof, look at the cross. Let go of those feelings and let the forgiveness of God cleanse your soul. Faith says it's worth the risk. Let God throw a party on your behalf.

I'm Not Who You Say I Am

A part of being human is reliving the past. At family gatherings, we tell old stories. They usually start with, "Do you remember when…" Most of us wander back to the past only from time to time. Others, however, never get out of the past. They are stuck there. Time has marched on, yet in their minds, time stopped for them at a significant event that happened long ago. Whatever it was, it continues to have such a strong hold on them they can't move forward or live in the present. They've allowed the sins of their past to define who they are today.

In Romans 5:19, what did Adam's act of disobedience make all of us?

What does Jesus's act of obedience make us?

In Christ, a believer has been made righteous as a gift of grace. What does a person miss knowing and experiencing if they continue to identify themselves by a past sin?

What is their real problem—forgiving themselves or recognizing their new identity in Christ?

Those who define themselves by a past sin normally keep this identity secret. In your opinion, why is this so? What is their fear?

How does this fear keep them from the love of God according to John 3:19-20?

Why is it important to live by the truth found in John 3:21?

What does a sinner become through faith in Jesus according to John 1:12?

How does the Holy Spirit confirm this truth to us in Romans 8:15-16?

> You are forever connected to the love of Jesus Christ. Nothing can separate you from his love. You are a forgiven, totally loved child of God.

God is rifling his grace right at you. Don't miss it. Open your heart and let his forgiveness pour in and free you from your past. Let his grace rip away the guilt and shame. Let his love set you on the path of genuinely living out who you are in Jesus Christ.

10

Rest

What if you're not growing in Christ? Is there a reason? Joe, from the story in the book, wasn't growing because he was so pre-occupied with changing his wife in order to salvage his marriage. He missed the message God had for him—the total forgiveness of sins. It was time for him to rest in Christ's finished work on the cross.

In 2 Peter 1:8-9, what qualities should a believer see increasing in his/her life?

What keeps a person from having these in increasing measure?

How does Peter describe people who have forgotten they have been cleansed from their sins?

How does God see you as a believer according to Colossians 1:22?

Do you believe that is true, or are you still worried that God might punish you for your sins?

Are you willing to accept that God's justice was fully satisfied in Christ and rest in the truth that you stand before him "holy in his sight, without blemish and free from accusation?"

Satisfied

God's justice was fully satisfied in the shed blood of Jesus. The biblical word is "propitiation." When was the last time you used that word in a sentence? It's not a word we hear very often, if at all. But it packs a powerful punch when it comes to our relationship with Jesus Christ.

What is the truth about man in Romans 3:23?

What did God do for us as a gift of grace? (vs 24)

This justification came through the redemption that is in Christ Jesus. How did this redemption come about? (vs 25)

What characteristic of God did this demonstrate to us? (vs 26)

When it comes to your sins, was God just in dealing with them in Christ?

Was he just as well in justifying you, the one who has faith in Jesus?

The word "propitiation" means to satisfy. Jesus fully satisfied the demands of God's justice and holiness. What does this say to you concerning the wrath (punishment) you justly deserved?

Since God is fully satisfied with the work of Christ, can you rest in his shed blood as complete and final payment for your sins?

God is satisfied. That's grace. The belief part is directly related to your answer to this question: Are you satisfied with the work of Jesus on your behalf?

What is the encouragement Jesus gives to those who are weary and burdened in Matthew 11:28?

What is his promise?

How did the writer of Hebrews word this promise in Hebrews 4:9?

> God is satisfied. Jesus's work achieved its purpose. This is grace. Jesus accomplished for you what you could not accomplish yourself.

He Sat Down

If you are satisfied with the work of Christ on your behalf, you've taken the first step to experiencing this rest. If you are still wrestling with this idea, here is further proof to help you along the way.

According to Hebrews 10:11, how did the Levites perform their religious duties?

How often did they carry out these duties?

Were the sacrifices they offered successful in taking away the sins of the people?

How would you like to be born into that bloodline?

In contrast, what did Jesus do after he provided purification for sins in Hebrews 1:3?

Why do you think he sat down?

When it comes to the sin issue, is there a need for Jesus to get up from his seated position according to Hebrews 7:27? Why?

In Hebrews 10:12, what did Christ offer?

What time frame did Christ's sacrifice cover?

Once he offered himself as final and complete payment for sin, what did he do?

What does this mean to you in regard to all your efforts to appease God and turn aside his wrath?

What does it mean for you to fully trust in Christ's work in Hebrews 4:10?

Have you entered God's rest?

The message is clear and strong. Jesus sat down because his work was finished. He accomplished everything the Father sent him to accomplish. He satisfied the justice and holiness of God. He satisfied his Father once and for all. He successfully turned aside the wrath of God.

The Justifier

God is just. He dealt with our sin. He didn't sweep it under the heavenly carpet. He judged it, he condemned it, and he punished it. But that was not the end goal.

God is both just and the justifier. He freely justifies "those who have faith in Jesus" (Romans 3:26). That includes you.

In Romans 4:3, when Abraham believed God, what did God credit to Abraham's account?

Is this righteousness something that Abraham merited through

Can we earn this righteousness?

Who are the ones that God justifies? (vs 5)

When you trust Christ, what was your faith credited as? (vs 5)

Where did this righteousness come from according to Philippians 3:9?

Was this righteousness derived through the law or through faith in Christ?

Do you think there is a righteousness that exceeds the righteousness that comes from God?

Since God has declared you righteous, what does that say to you concerning the forgiveness of your sins?

What would happen to the righteousness that was credited to your account if only one of your sins was left unpunished?

What is the result of being justified with faith in Romans 5:1?

Because of Christ's work on your behalf, what is true of you according to Romans 8:1?

The fact that God has declared us righteous in his sight is proof that all our sins have been forgiven. On the basis of Jesus's shed blood, God treats us as if we had never sinned.

The fact that God has declared you righteous in his sight is proof that all your sins have been forgiven. When I say all, I mean sins of the past, present and future. They have been sent away from you as far as the east is from the west, and righteousness was credited to your account.

The work has been done. It is time to rest and enjoy your freedom in Christ. That's what we will examine in part three. Spoiler alert. The good news keeps getting better.

11

You Are Free

Forgiveness plus life equals freedom. Real freedom.

This is where the Gospel takes us. Paul put it this way: "It is for freedom that Christ has set us free" (Galatians 5:1). Freedom is what you have longed for all of your life. Now in Christ, it is yours.

But what does it mean to be free?

In Galatians 5:1, why did Christ set you free?

How are we to stand in response to this truth?

What must we guard against as believers in Christ?

Are there voices out there that say to you, "you can't handle freedom?"

In your opinion, how do you stand firm against those voices?

Legalism:
Anything man does to earn God's love and
acceptance. A works-based approach to God.

Here is the good news of the Gospel. Through faith in Jesus we have
escaped the world and it's system. We are not under law. We are
under grace. We've been set free. This is God's goal for us, and he has
equipped us to handle it. This was foreshadowed in one of the most
familiar stories in the Old Testament.

A Plot Gone Bad

Hatred and jealousy are powerful forces. They can make a person do
unthinkable acts. But they can't thwart God's plans or his purpose.

In Genesis 15:13, what did God say was going to happen to
Abraham's descendants?

Who was the first of Abraham's descendants to be sent to Egypt?
(Genesis 37:28)

Why did Joseph's brothers sell him to the Midianites according to
Genesis 37:11?

Joseph rose from slave to ruler because he correctly interpreted
Pharaoh's troubling dream. How specifically did Pharaoh reward
Joseph in Genesis 41:41?

Climate change, in the form of a drought and famine, devastated the Middle East during those times. This catastrophe was the heart of Pharaoh's troubling dream. With Joseph in charge of the land, Egypt was prepared to handle the famine. They were so well prepared, who else were Joseph and Egypt able to help in Genesis 41:57?

What did Jacob, Joseph's father, tell his other sons to do in Genesis 42:2-5?

What did God say to Jacob in a vision in Genesis 46:3-4?

With God's encouragement and guidance, what did Jacob and his descendants do in Genesis 46:6-7?

How many of Jacob's family went to Egypt? (Genesis 46:27)

Joseph's brothers intended to harm him. But what was God's purpose through this story according to Genesis 50:20?

After they settled in the land, what happened to them in Exodus 1:6?

Describe how the new king of Egypt dealt with the Israelites in Exodus 1:8-14.

Why did the Egyptians deal with the Israelites in this way?

Pharaoh feared what the Israelites might do if they continued to grow in number. This fear led him to oppress them through control and slavery. Have you experienced these types of negative forces trying to rob you of your freedom in Christ? Explain.

According to Exodus 12:40, how long did the Israelites live in Egypt?

For four hundred years, just as God had said, the Israelites suffered at the hands of the Egyptians. They were living in the wrong place, under the control of the wrong person, carrying out the wrong purpose. But God did not leave them there. Freedom was his plan. He heard their cries and elevated one from within their ranks to lead them to freedom.

A Powerful Promise

Moses was that man. God revealed his plan to rescue his people to Moses when he appeared to him in a burning bush.

How did God introduce himself to Moses in Exodus 3:6?

How did Moses respond?

According to Exodus 3:8, why did God come down?

Who was God's choice to lead the people out of Egypt? (Exodus 3:10)

Was Moses confident that God had made the right choice? (Exodus 3:11)

How did God clear away Moses' doubts? (Exodus 3:12)

What was the name of this God who was going to be with his people according to Exodus 3:14?

Let's stop right here for a moment. The Israelites world was about to be rocked. God was about to sever them from the only life they had ever known. Every step of the way would be a step into the unknown. Granted, they wanted to be free. There was only one way. I AM WHO I AM would lead the charge. He was their hope.

In what way is I AM WHO I AM your hope today in Colossians 1:27?

If Jesus was not in your life, would you have any hope of living in freedom?

Jesus Christ delivered you out of darkness. He set you free by unlocking the chains of sin and death that held you captive. He didn't leave you to figure out this newfound freedom on your own. He came to live inside you. Your hope of living life to the full is anchored to his power and presence in you. This hope trumps fear. And it silences all those legalistic voices, both the internal and external ones, that say you can't handle freedom. Christ in you says you can!

The Exodus

Pharaoh was stubborn. He was not going to let the Israelites go. They were far too valuable to him and the Egyptian economy. Through a series of plagues, God displayed his awesome power. And with each one, Pharaoh's heart hardened even more. It was the last plague, which we know as the Passover, that compelled Pharaoh to let the Israelites go.

What were God's instructions to the people concerning the Passover? (Exodus 12:3, 6-7)

On that same night, God was going to pass through the land. What two things was he going to do? (Exodus 12:12)

What was his promise to the Israelites? (Exodus 12:13)

After the Lord passed through the land, how did Pharaoh respond in Exodus 12:31-32?

Six hundred thousand men, along with women and children, gathered up their belongings and all they had plundered from the Egyptians, and they left. How did the Lord lead them out of the land in Exodus 13:21-22?

Even though the Lord was with them, what overcame them when they looked back and saw Pharaoh's army chasing after them in Exodus 14:10?

When fear hits, we lose perspective on all that God has for us both now and in the future. In what ways do we see this happening with the Israelites in Exodus 14:11-12?

Standing on the shores of the Red Sea, the Israelites believed their end was near. How did God save them in Exodus 14:21?

Did they have anything to fear?

After they passed through the Red Sea on dry land, how did they respond to God? (Exodus 14:30-31)

> Your old way of life has come to an end.
> You are no longer a slave to sin.
> You are a child of the living God.
> But not just a child. God declared you to be a son.

Three Lessons for Us

What does this story tell us today?

First, it tells us that salvation is God's work from start to finish. Every aspect of Israel's rescue was carried out by God alone. His power and presence delivered them to safety and freedom.

Explain in your own words how God's presence and power set you free.

Next, Israel's old way of life came to an end.

The Egyptian army drowned in the Red Sea. What does this say about their rule and reign over the Israelites?

Who now would shape and order their lives?

Do you see the pattern of the Exodus story in Romans 6:5-7?

What have you been set free from?

What does this mean about your old way of life?

What did God declare you to be in Galatians 4:6?

How does God confirm this truth to you?

Since you are no longer a slave to sin, but God's child, what else did God make you? (Galatians 4:7)

Who now is shaping and ordering your life as a child of God?

In his presence is there anything to fear?

Yes, freedom can be scary. Everything in the world tries to keep you from it. Even your old legalistic thoughts discourage you from walking that path. Be brave and courageous. Freedom is what you have longed for. It's yours. Every step you take in this new way of life, remember this; he is there with you.

12

Don't Look Back

"New" is an exciting word when it's attached to things like cars, clothes, a house and gadgets. But when it comes to the weightier matters of life, "new" can be a scary word. It means change. It means stepping into the unknown and the unfamiliar. This is hard for us. We resist with all our strength and might. This is just part of our human nature.

But here is the deal; the Gospel ushers us into the new. As we learned in the last chapter there is no going back. The only option is to move forward into all that God has for us in Jesus Christ.

What does Paul say about those who are in Christ in 2 Corinthians 5:17?

What has happened to the old?

What is now here?

In the following verses, list what is new for you in Christ.

Romans 6:4

John 1:12

Ephesians 4:24

Ezekiel 36:26

Hebrews 9:15

John 13:34

Romans 7:6

The world, the flesh and the devil will do everything possible to keep you from enjoying all that you have new. What does Peter say about that old way of life in 1 Peter 4:3?

What does moving forward in this new way of life mean to you according to 2 Corinthians 3:17?

The "new" that Christ has for you is better than anything you could ever dream or imagine. And besides, you can't go back. Once you are in the light, you can't go back to darkness. Once you have been set free, you will never be a slave to sin and death again. Once you cross over from death to life, the only way is forward in the newness of life.

A Tale of Two Kingdoms

Our story is a tale of two kingdoms. It involves a daring rescue mission that snatches us away from one kingdom and places us fully and forever into a new kingdom.

How does Paul describe this daring rescue mission in Colossians 1:13-14?

What kingdom do you now live in as a child of God?

What do you have in Christ?

How did God execute this plan according to John 1:4-5?

God's rescue plan was drawn up by love and grace and was carried out through death, burial and resurrection. How did Paul explain this plan in Romans 6:3-4?

God did all of this so that you might do what?

What is your ultimate destiny according to Romans 21:1-4?

Through faith in Jesus Christ, you have gone from darkness to light and from the power of Satan to God. You are in the kingdom of the Son.

> The kingdom of darkness has no hold over you anymore. The power of sin and death has been broken. You are free!

The Way of the Kingdom

Okay, so you've been raised to walk in the newness of life. How does that happen? What are the marks of this new life in Christ? Another way to ask these questions is this: What are the new "laws" of the Kingdom, the laws God placed in your mind and wrote on your heart? (Hebrews 8:10)

In Colossians 1:3-4, what had Paul heard concerning the believers in Colossae?

From what did their faith in Christ and their love for others spring? (Colossians 1:5)

Where did they hear about this hope?

What three qualities does the Gospel bring to a person's life?

What happens when the Gospel is met with faith, hope and love? (Colossians 1:6)

What did God do that guarantees your inheritance in Ephesians 1:13-14?

What will we find out about ourselves when Jesus appears in 1 John 3:2?

In what ways does this hope affect us here and now? (1 John 3:3)

Where does our faith come from according to Romans 10:17?

Based on this verse, does faith have any meaning apart from Jesus Christ?

How did Jesus define sin according to John 16:8-9?

When you lived in darkness, what then was the dominant principle that guided your life?

What happened to your heart of unbelief when you heard the good news concerning Jesus Christ?

This radical change equipped you for life in the kingdom of Christ. What does this life look like according to Galatians 2:20?

How is our faith in Jesus Christ expressed in Galatians 5:6?

Hope anchors us to Jesus, and to all that we are and have in Him. From this hope spring forth faith and love. These three—faith, hope and love—are the way of the kingdom.

Press On

One of the lessons of life is that we can't go back. The only option is to move forward. The same is true for the Christian life. Once we are saved, we can't go back. We can't reverse all that Christ accomplished. We can't go from life back to death. And we can't go from belief back to unbelief. Why would we want to?

In Romans 6:2, what does Paul say has happened with us regarding our relationship to sin?

Since this is true, what question does Paul raise for us to consider?

You died to sin, to unbelief. The old you is gone. You are new in Jesus, equipped to live a life of faith, hope, and love. What does the Scripture say to you? Press on!

What is the encouragement for you to take hold of in 1 Timothy 6:12?

What was Paul's attitude about his new life in Christ? (Philippians 3:13-14)

Is there anything holding you back from taking hold of this eternal life to which you were called, or pressing on toward the goal?

Are you fearful of the unknown?

Are you concerned about what other people will think of you?

Do you think the world has something better to offer?

Are you willing to cast these aside and trust confidently in the one who loved you and gave himself for you?

Pressing on. It takes courage, but experiencing the life of Jesus is worth everything. This is what he saved you for.

13

Living a Sunday Life in a Friday World

The wonderful S.M. Lockridge delivered the powerful and moving sermon titled, "It's Friday, but Sunday's Coming." If you ever hear it, you will never forget it. It's a sermon that fills that darkest day with light and hope. Sunday is here. Jesus walked out of that tomb and he lives today. This is the good-news story.

Have you come to know this story? Has your dark, hopeless Friday come to an end—the searching, the restlessness, the emptiness, the guilt and shame? Have you found what you are looking for in the person of Jesus Christ? Has he given you new life?

If so, the resurrection story has become your story. Sunday is here for you. Like Jesus, you've walked out of your spiritual tomb fully alive—raised to walk in the newness of life here and now. Sunday has arrived for you, but not for the world. It's still Friday for this world of darkness.

This raises an important question: How do you live a Sunday life in a Friday world?

In the World

"We are in the world but not of the world" is a popular saying in Christian circles. Although it is not in the Bible, it does summarize what the Bible says on the subject. Let's take a look.

In John 17:11, even though Jesus would not remain in this world, what did he say about his disciples?

What was his prayer for them and for what purpose?

What is the disposition of the world toward those who have been given the Word of God in John 17:14-17? Why is this so?

What is the world's disposition toward you?

What is Jesus's prayer on your behalf?

In John 17:17, how specifically will God protect you from the evil one?

How are we to live in this world according to 1 Peter 2:11?

Based on who you are in Christ, do you fit in with the world anymore?

When the Bible speaks of the world, it doesn't mean planet earth. It is referring to the world system. In 1 John 2:16, what makes up this world system?

What does John say will happen to the world and its desires in 1 John 2:17?

What about those who do the will of God?

This world system had its genesis in the garden at the tree of the knowledge of good and evil. Mankind has been feeding on that tree ever since. How does that look in a religious setting according to Matthew 6:5?

How did Paul describe this attitude in Romans 10:3-4?

In Romans 10:3-4, Paul draws the line between the way of the world and the way of Christ. It is the difference between law and grace. Resurrection life is lived by grace through faith. Since that is the case, you may ask what then is the purpose of the law?

> The law can't save us. That is Jesus's job.
> The law points us to him.

The Real Reason

The law diagnoses our spiritual problem, but it cannot provide the cure. That's Jesus's job.

Is it possible for you to be declared righteous in God's sight by the works of the law according to Romans 3:20?

On the contrary, what happens through the law?

What does Galatians 3:24-25 say is the purpose of the law?

Once faith has come, has the law fulfilled its purpose in you?

Is there any further need for you to be under the law?

To the Galatians who were still arguing that the law was indeed the rule for life, Paul had some sobering words: "You foolish Galatians." Even though they started with the Spirit, how were they trying to finish according to Galatians 3:2-3?

Here is what we need to know. Law as a rule of life rests squarely on the shoulders of human effort. What are some of the problems this way of life causes?

Galatians 1:6

Galatians 1:7

Galatians 1:10

Galatians 2:12

Galatians 2:13

Galatians 2:14

Galatians 2:21

Galatians 4:9

Galatians 5:1

Galatians 5:13

Galatians 5:15

The law has a purpose and that is to show you your need for Christ. But that purpose does not supersede God's greater purpose for you. How does Paul explain this greater purpose in Galatians 3:17-18?

What was God's promise according to Galatians 3:14?

Romans 7:6 says you have been released from the law. For what purpose?

Now you live in the new way of the Spirit. What was the old way?

By the Spirit

The first step in living a Sunday life in a Friday world is to let go of human effort. The Sunday life is a life of faith. It is a life that is led by and empowered by the Spirit of God.

What is Paul's encouragement to you concerning how you are to live as a child of God in Galatians 5:16?

What is the result of walking by the Spirit?

Let's put some handles on what it means to walk by the Spirit. In Romans 5:5, what has been poured in your heart and by whom?

Would you say that God's love and the desires of the flesh stand in opposition to each other?

Concerning this love, how does the Spirit impress this love in your inner being in Ephesians 3:16-19?

Is this knowledge of God's love merely intellectual in nature?

What is the result of the work of God's Spirit on this front for you in Ephesians 3:19?

If you are filled to the measure with the fullness of God, what will be expressed through you?

How is our faith expressed according to Galatians 5:6?

If you are expressing the love of God to others by faith (walking by the Spirit), at that moment will you be gratifying the desires of the flesh?

How does Peter describe "walking by the Spirit" in 2 Peter 1:3-4?

Will you sometimes get off course as far as walking by the Spirit is concerned?

Even so, what is God's promise to you in Philippians 1:6?

Walking by the Spirit is the Sunday life. Who is the source of this life according to Philippians 2:12-13?

Walking by the Spirit—that's Sunday living in a Friday world.

> Living by the Spirit is trusting God
> to complete the work he began in you.

14

The Goal

Knowing God's will is one of our deepest desires, yet it can be one of our most frustrating quests.

Most people think of "God's will" in terms of God's plan for them. They want to know how to choose whom to marry, where to live, and what to do in life. For many, finding God's perfect plan for them is like finding that proverbial needle in a haystack. With this idea about "God's will," many believers get stuck in the mud with decisions because they are so afraid they might miss what God has in store for them.

Let's debunk that right now. Being stuck in the mud and afraid to make a decision is not God's will. He has called you to a life of freedom, one that is built on the foundation of God's promise in Romans 8:28: "We know that in all things God works for the good of those who love him, who have been called according to his purpose." This is a win-win proposition. But to get there, we need to shift our thinking regarding God's will.

The Shift

Instead of thinking of God's will in terms of a plan, let's shift gears and look at it in terms of a legal will. God has a will like that and it is called the New Covenant.

What did the prophet Jeremiah say would happen at some point in the future? (Jeremiah 32:31)

God prepared his will for his people in advance. But what has to happen before a will goes into effect according to Hebrews 9:16?

Whose death made this New Covenant effective?

When did this New Covenant begin?

What covenant was in place for Israel before Christ died?

How did Christ announce this New Covenant to his disciples in Luke 22:20?

In Hebrews 8:10-12, what are the four provisions of the New Covenant?

In reading these four provisions, what do you see as God's desire and goal for you?

When did the New Covenant begin?
At the cross. Jesus's death changed everything.

Don't underestimate the far reach of these promises where your life in Christ is concerned. These contain everything you need for life and godliness. In the New Covenant, you can live life to the full, which is God's will for you. He has rescued you through Christ and delivered you to this end.

Be Perfect

Telos is a Greek word that has philosophical roots extending back to Plato and Aristotle. The word refers to an end or a purpose. Plato and Aristotle believed that there were ends or purposes to which all of life was leading. In other words, what happens in the world is not accidental. There is a propelling force moving the world to a stated end.

Telos also has biblical roots and it is a word that is significant in telling the Gospel story. The first time we see it in the New Testament is in the Sermon on the Mount.

What is Jesus's command to us in Matthew 5:48?

What is the standard of perfection that Jesus calls us to?

When you read these words to be perfect, what do you think Jesus is expecting from you?

Most of us equate perfection with being flawless or not having any defects. The word telos, which is our word "perfect", conveys a different meaning. One of its meanings is "wanting for nothing." It's a place of contentment. How does this meaning change the reading of Matthew 5:48?

If Jesus calls you to perfection, how are you to reach that goal?

Based on Hebrews 7:11,18-19, is obedience to the law the path that will lead you to perfection? Why or why not?

How does the writer of Hebrews describe the law In Hebrews 7:18?

What did God do with the law because of its weakness?

In Hebrews 10:10,14, what does the writer say is true of you?

What made you holy and perfect forever?

As a result, where do you now stand according to Romans 5:1-2?

Jesus cleansed you, made you holy, and then delivered you smack-dab in the center of God's will, right where you belong.

> The law can't deliver you to the goal. Only grace can do that. What the law was powerless to do, Christ did.

A Declaration

Are you ready to make a declaration?

God in his grace and mercy delivered you into the New Covenant. That is where he wanted you to be, and that is where you are. Because of Christ, you will never be outside of God's favor. You are in the New Covenant and there is no turning back.

God equipped Paul to be a minister of what according to 2 Corinthian 3:6?

Is this ministry of the letter or of the Spirit?

What is the difference between the two?

Since the Spirit gives life, what then is God's goal for you in the New Covenant?

What else is at the center of this New Covenant in 2 Corinthians 3:17?

Which covenant do you want to live in—the Old or the New?

Are you willing today to declare this: I am New Covenant?

It's time to fully embrace God's perfect plan and will for you. It's time to say, "I am a new-covenant believer."

The Work of Grace

Grace is powerful and active. It is not passive or reactive in the least. Grace is proactive. It is Jesus Christ living his life in you. He saved you by grace through faith. And now by grace he is perfecting that faith, bringing it to maturity.

As we have learned, God is completing the work he began in each one of us (Philippians 1:6). This process happens in the trials of life.

In John 16:33, what did Jesus say was going to happen in this world?

Even so, what is possible for you to have in Christ?

Why?

Through the trials of life, you learn that Jesus is enough. You learn that his grace is sufficient.

How does James encourage you to face trials? (James 1:2)

What is the end result of these various trials in James 1:3-4?

Describe how this process of maturity through trials unfolds in Romans 5:3-5.

What does Peter say we learn about our faith through the various trials we encounter in 1 Peter 1:6-9?

When we endure hardship as discipline, what can we expect as a result in Hebrews 12:7-11?

How did God answer Paul's prayer in 2 Corinthians 12:8-9?

Made perfect—there is our word again. What is made perfect through our weaknesses?

What did this truth cause Paul to do concerning his weaknesses in 2 Corinthians 12:9-10?

Admitting weakness is hard to do. Sometimes in life, we believe we are strong enough to handle what life throws our way. We try to take the bull by the horns. Has this ever happened in your life? What was the result?

Are you willing to boast in your weakness, so that Christ's power will rest on you?

What will you discover about yourself when you are weak? (2 Corinthians 12:10)

Jesus is enough. He is more than adequate for any circumstance or problem. Abide in him. Trust him. Experience the full measure of his resurrected life. This is where God's grace takes you. This is New Covenant living.

15

Eternal Life

Life is about relationships. Knowing and being known.

This is at the heart of eternal life.

How did Jesus define eternal life in John 17:3?

What stunning compliment is given to those who are called children of God in 1 John 4:17?

How does knowing God shape you and conform you to the image of Christ?

What can we boast about as New Covenant believers in Hebrews 8:11?

God took away your sins, reconciled you to himself, justified you, sanctified you, made you alive, and poured his Spirit into your life for this single purpose—to know and enjoy him. This is ultimate freedom. This is eternal life.

> "God created men to know Him.
> God created men to enjoy Him." Dan DeHaan

The Relationship

Why did Jesus come to earth? There are several different biblical answers to this question. For this study, let's focus on one that weaves its way through John's writings.

Who is the only person that has ever seen God according to John 1:18?

So is it possible for us to really know what God is like without someone telling us?

What does Jesus do for us concerning God the Father?

After Jesus made the startling claim that he was the way, the truth and the life, Philip said, "Lord, show us the Father and that will be enough for us." How did Jesus respond to this request in John 14:9?

What does the writer of Hebrews reveal about Jesus in Hebrews 1:3?

How did Paul describe Jesus in Colossians 1:15?

Who do you turn to find out the truth about God the Father?

In Athens, Paul saw this inscription on an altar: "To an unknown God" (Acts 17:23). If you were tasked with answering this inscription, how would you make the unknown God known?

Earlier in your life, God was unknown to you. At that time, what did you think that he was like? How did you describe God? What did you suppose he thought about you?

How have your answers changed now that Jesus has revealed the Father to you?

Only in Jesus is God the Father made known to man.

God initiated this relationship with you. He reached down to you through Jesus Christ. That's grace. His grace worked in you a desire to know him. That's faith. At God's initiative, a union was formed— you in Christ and Christ in you. That was the point when eternal life began for you, when God started making himself known to you in a real and personal way.

Children, Young Men, and Fathers

God is an infinite being. We are finite. He reveals himself to us more and more as we are ready to receive. Our knowledge of him grows over time. Our initial, incomplete knowledge grows into a fuller or more complete knowledge. John sketches out this progression in his first letter by addressing children, young men and fathers.

> To the new believer: Your sins are forgiven, and you are a child of God. You belong. You are in the family.

In 1 John 2:12, 14, what two things did John say to children?

What do these statements tell you about the character of God and his desire for you?

How does God reveal to you that he is your Father in Galatians 4:6?

If you are a new believer, based on these verses, what two truths does God want you to know about him?

> To the young men: Through your knowledge of God, you are overcoming the evil one and learning to live as a child of light in this world of darkness.

If you are in ministry, what two truths are critical for new believers to know?

What is true of young men according to 1 John 2:13-14?

What is the result of being strong and having the word of God live in you?

The arguments and lofty pretensions of the world set themselves up against what according to 2 Corinthians 10:5?

Based on the above verse, what is it that will enable you to overcome the arguments and philosophies of the world?

What did John say about fathers in 1 John 2:13-14?

To the fathers: God's love for the world has become yours.

This is very similar to the statement John made to children. How would a father's knowledge of God differ from that of a child?

Think about a long-term relationship you have enjoyed. What do you know about that person now that you did not know when the relationship started? How has that knowledge strengthened and enriched the relationship? How has that knowledge changed you?

What do you now know about God the Father that you did not know when you first trusted Jesus? How has that knowledge changed you?

As you grow in Christ, are you seeing that God is aligning your heart with his and giving you a broader perspective of his grand purposes in the world?

The purpose of grace is to connect you to the love of God. It is Jesus who makes this love known to you. He places on your eyes a lens of grace that brings the truth that God is love into clear focus.

A New Command

The grace of God is not without its critics. This doesn't make sense. How could any believer in Christ be critical of the very reality that saved him and now sustains him? Yet many believers are. They drone away about taking grace too far and using it as a license to sin. They say grace needs to be balanced by law. That is not God's plan. God's plan is "by grace through faith." This is the balance God strikes in us. It's a balance that connects us to a new command.

> One of the criticisms of the grace of God is that it leaves people without law, or a rule for life. How does the first promise of the New Covenant address this criticism? (Hebrews 8:10)

> What does God put in our minds and write on our hearts according to the following verses:

> *Romans 3:27*

> *1 Peter 1:3*

> *I John 3:23*

> What happens when there is a change of the priesthood according to Hebrews 7:12?

Who is now our high priest according to Hebrews 5:10?

So was there a change in the priesthood?

As a result, what else had to change?

> The Holy Spirit works in you to animate your faith, anchor your hope and source your love. He has lifted you out of that old way and ordered your steps to walk in love.

How do the New Testament writers describe this new law in the following verses?

Romans 8:2

Galatians 6:2

James 1:25

Who is the source of this New Covenant way of life according to 2 Corinthians 3:3?

What is John's encouragement to you in 1 John 4:7?

Where does he say love comes from?

What is true of those who love others according to John?

What is the mark that distinguishes you from the world and is the evidence that you are a disciple of Jesus Christ according to John 13:34-35?

> To know God is to know that he is love.

You have been entrusted with the knowledge of God. That's what distinguishes you from the world. That's the story of the Gospel.

True Freedom

True freedom allows us to know and to be known. It also enables us to be generous and to look toward the needs of others.

What were we called to according to Galatians 5:13?

How are we to use our freedom as children of God?

Consider the apostle Peter. He denied the Lord three times. Yet, Jesus lifted him out of his despair. That's grace.

How specifically did Jesus restore Peter in John 21:15-17?

How did this love of God work in Peter's heart to feed God's sheep in the Gentile world in Acts 10:28-29; Acts 11:15-18?

Peter knew the Lord. The love of God compelled him to break away from long-held sentiments toward the Gentiles and tell them about Jesus. How has your heart knowledge of God transformed you and enabled you to reach out and serve others in love?

As you grow in your knowledge of Christ, what do you become like in this world of darkness according to Philippians 2:15-16?

The gift of grace is Jesus Christ. You have the joy and privilege of knowing him and walking in his love. You have the privilege of making him known in this world of darkness.

Ae you ready to take hold of this eternal life? Are you ready for God to align your heart with his? Are you ready to grow in your knowledge of Jesus Christ? If so. get ready for the adventure of a lifetime. You will soon find that there is nothing better than knowing Jesus Christ. He is your life.

Rejoice. In Christ you know the God of the universe. Even more amazing, the God of the universe knows you. And as Jesus said, this is eternal life.

Epilogue

Near the end of his life, Paul summoned the leaders of the Ephesian church to meet with him. It would be their last time together. He let the leaders know he was going to Jerusalem. Everyone knew this meant trouble for him—hardships and possible imprisonment. Yet he was compelled by the Spirit to go. He was going to carry out the task God had given him to do.

In Acts 20:24, what did Paul say was his mission in life?

What was his desire concerning this mission?

What does he equate the good news to?

Is there any good news apart from the grace of God?

There is no good news apart from the grace of God.
The simple gospel is simply grace.

How did Paul bless these leaders as he was departing from them
in Acts 20:32?

Why did he commit them to the word of God's grace?

Paul was not the only apostle given the task of testifying to the
grace of God. How did Peter conclude his first letter in 1 Peter
5:12?

What is his encouragement to you concerning this grace of God?

Can you think of a better place to stand?

What is his encouragement to you in 2 Peter 3:18?

Based on these two passages in Peter's letters, what is God's
greatest desire for you as a child of God?

In the coming ages, how is God going to show the incomparable
riches of his grace?

Grace is the way of salvation. Grace is the way of the Christian life.
Grace will stand as an eternal testimony to all creation.

As for you, grace opened the door to everything new. Through faith in Jesus and his finished work, you've walked through. You've taken your stand. Now grow in grace and the knowledge of Jesus Christ. As Paul encouraged Timothy, "Fight the good fight of the faith. Take hold of the eternal life to which you were called" (1 Timothy 6:12). This is how the Christian life works. And it's all yours in abundance by grace through faith.

> Nothing can award the heart true fulfillment, deep joy, or genuine contentment like the grace of God. His favor brings the purest and truest sense of happiness to the soul.

An Invitation

It is my prayer that this book has pointed you to Jesus Christ and to the wonders of his love and grace. If you have received Jesus Christ through reading Simple Gospel Simply Grace, if your life has been impacted in other ways, or if you would like to learn more about the ministry of Basic Gospel, please let me know. I would love to hear from you. Please write to me. My address is:

Bob Christopher
Basic Gospel
751 Hebron Parkway
Suite 310
Lewisville, TX 75057

Or you can send an e-mail to bob@basicgospel.net

May God's grace be with you in abundance!

Simple Gospel, Simply Grace

"We're all natural-born legalists," says author Bob Christopher. "We try to live for God, but it's impossible to do."

Why? Because all our efforts and ideas are based on the same fear-based, guilt-driven plot line: Try harder. As you've undoubtedly noticed, it just doesn't work.

Simple Gospel, Simply Grace showcases an alternative, which is actually God's original plan: Everything you're trying to achieve in the Christian life has already been given to you—from God, by grace, in Christ.

Simple Gospel

How Your Christian Life is Really Supposed to Work

Simply Grace

Bob Christopher

Do you struggle to receive what God has freely given? How can you begin to experience true freedom, assurance of your forgiveness, and victory over sin? How can the power that raised Jesus from the dead enable you to live and love the way He did?

You'll discover the answers in this crystal-clear portrayal of the simple gospel—which is simply grace.

Order the book and study guide at simplegospelsimplygrace.com or call 844.412.2742 - toll free

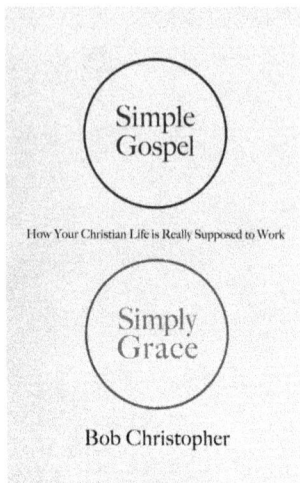

Connect with Bob Christopher

Twitter: @rcchristopherjr

Facebook: fb.com/bob.christopher

Blog: bobchristopher.net

Email: bob@basicgospel.net

BASIC GOSPEL
Hear it. Believe it. Live it.

The Gospel of Jesus Christ is simple, powerful, and life changing. It declares the love of God for mankind. It is the good news people long to hear. Radio delivers it straight to the heart.

Every weekday, the Basic Gospel radio team is on the air fielding tough questions from listeners around the world and delivering practical biblical truth, encouragement and hope to help them grow in Jesus Christ. The 30-minute Basic Gospel program is grace oriented and biblically uncompromised. It's where the love of Jesus Christ intersects with daily life.

Join your hosts, Bob Christopher, Richard Peifer, and Bob Davis each weekday at 3 p.m. CT. Call the program with your questions: 844.322.2742 - toll free

For stations, archives, podcast, and resources to help you in your Christian life, please visit:

BASICGOSPEL.NET

"I got saved listening to this radio program. I was empty and close to suicide, very close to suicide. I was listening to this station, to every program there day and night. But there was one that caught my attention. I was searching. I was like at the end of the rope. I said to God, 'I can't do this anymore.' I found answers through this ministry. Keep preaching the grace of God."

BASICGOSPEL
Hear it. Believe it. Live it.

basicgospel.net